BEYOND THE EYE

Printed by Amazon KDP.
Design by Tasmin Briers.

First published 2021.

BEYOND THE EYE

Jema Fowler

Acknowledgements

I have learned so much from the research and studies of neuroscientist Joe Dispenza. His teaching and courses are incredibly eye-opening, informative and have taught me everything I know about the field of possibility and life. I'm very grateful for the work he has published, and so I give a big thank you to him and Tasmin Briers for helping me bring this book to life.

THE STATE
OF YOUR LIFE
IS NOTHING
MORE THAN A
REFLECTION
OF YOUR STATE
OF MIND.

Dr Wayne Dyer

Introduction

Hello lovely readers; I hope you are all well and that 2020 hasn't disheartened you too much. *Beyond the Eye* is the follow up to my debut book *Beyond the Mind* that was published earlier this year during the coronavirus lockdown. It was the first book to be released within this self-help series and it's an important step towards your road to manifesting, taking a leap of faith, and letting go of negativity.

In *Beyond the Eye*, we cover some new ground and look at the impact of the Universe. We look at the way that our mind and how we think controls our emotions. It takes you through the stages of mindfulness, how to practise it every day and how to create positive habits to benefit your happiness. In my first book, we talked about 'manifesting', and so many of you wanted to know more and how it works — "What is manifesting? How do I manifest? How do I be mindful in everyday life?"

This is where *Beyond the Eye* was born!

The road to manifesting might be new to some of you, but it doesn't need to be complicated... Meditation and mindfulness will help you feel, think and be more positive. It will help you regain control of your own mind rather than letting it control you.

Creating positive habits and learning how to control our thoughts will encourage you to see your life in a more mindful way. Utilising the tools of meditation and manifesting that I teach through my books can help open your eyes and realize that only you decide how you feel. **Do not let your thoughts run away with you!**

In this book, I want to teach you about the Law of Attraction and how you can use the Universe to help you get to where you want to be. When someone says 'it is written in your stars', it *really* is.

I'm going to explain to you how the Universe works, and how you can indulge in scientific energy to attract positivity and happiness into your life. This knowledge in combination with the idea of manifesting will help you make these practices work *for* you, not against you.

Since my first book, I have studied a course in quantum science to ensure that my readers are confident that everything in this book is scientifically backed — it *definitely* works. Whether you are simply curious about the Universe you live in and want to find out more or you plan to actively use the suggestions in this book, *Beyond the Eye* will help you understand your own mind and emotions.

Consider *Beyond the Eye* a short guide on the impact of self-control and how to understand the Law of Attraction on a scientific level. It will help bring you content and calm in your everyday life. Beauty is in the eye of the beholder and now, happiness is too.

I hope you love *Beyond the Eye*, and that you look forward to more books in this series in the future!

MANY PEOPLE
ARE ALIVE... BUT
DON'T TOUCH
THE MIRACLE
OF BEING
ALIVE.

Thich Nhat Hanh

CHAPTER 1

What We See vs. Reality

This is a subject that is very important, not only in the physical world and our interactions, but in our virtual world on the Internet. If you take anything away from this book, let it be that you need to take a step back from technology and social media. The sooner we realise that not everything we see and read is true, the sooner we can become fulfilled in our own lives and happiness.

Most of the content that we see on these social media platforms are not what we (or even they) would call 'your average day.' The carefully curated photographs we see online of sports cars, luxury holidays and £10,000 give-aways are often backed purely on sponsors, corporate companies or rented products. These are the methods used to entice us into the Instagram post and the products, but just because it exists does not mean that it's real!

There is no denying that as a professional job, influencing works — it's great for business and it's great to increase exposure. But from a personal perspective, it can set you up for having unrealistic expectations of how successful you are or how you should be living your life.

If you live in this constant state of comparison, it will only leave you feeling low, unworthy or not as good as the people you see online who seem to 'have it all.' It might be that you love designer clothes, makeup and handbags as well, or *really* need of the Bali holiday everyone seems to be on. But social media influencing is a business and it's really easy to forget that!

Just because you don't have 50,000 followers on Instagram or a Lamborghini with a modelling contract by 30 does not mean you have failed. This is why it is important that we learn to look at life with clarity and mindfulness. Comparison is the thief of joy.

But that's not what I'm here to talk about.

Whilst *Beyond the Eye* doesn't intend to dwell on the impact of social media, it's important to understand how you spend your time and the way it can impact your mood. Comparing yourself to the unattainable lifestyles of strangers and digital business people is only going to rob you of self-esteem and confidence. If you judge a fish by its ability to climb a tree, it will live its whole life believing that it is stupid.

Centre yourself outside of the social media bubble by regularly practising mindfulness. It's a strong, successful method at providing clarity in your everyday life — **a strong mind leads a strong life.**

IT ALL BEGINS
AND ENDS IN
YOUR MIND.
WHAT YOU GIVE
POWER TO, HAS
POWER OVER
YOU.

Leon Brown

CHAPTER 2

Human Consciousness

Have you heard the term 'egocentric'? If not, this is what I mean:

To be egocentric means that we struggle to see or understand the views or opinions of other people. The American psychologist David Elkind described why it happens, referring to it as a 'heightened self-awareness and self-consciousness.'

Elkind says that when we are growing up, we feel as though our actions and behaviours are being judged. This has a knock-on effect on our behaviour because when we feel like we are being watched, our behaviour will change to adhere to how *we think* they want us to act. This continues throughout adulthood and it can eventually become what is called a 'self-focused trait' in our adult life and within our relationships.

Going by Elkind's ideas, a lot of us are considered to live in an egocentric state today. This can be encouraged by how we behave on social media — seeking approval from other people in the form of getting lots of likes on your Facebook posts or having lots of followers on Instagram.

To live the best version of ourselves, we need to try and get out of this frame of mind. There will be a massive change in your perception of yourself and everything else in the world once you realise the way that you act is impacting the way that you think.

***

By definition, the opposite of egocentric is altruistic. The dictionary definition of altruistic is *'showing a selfless concern for the well-being of others; similar to self-sacrificing and considerate'.* Once we get out of the habit of people-pleasing, we end up living truer to ourselves.

This 'genuineness' is a huge step in becoming a much more compassionate person. It helps you let go of some of the negative thinking habits that you have been giving energy to the whole way throughout your life without even realising.

Living in a more altruistic and empathetic way will change how we think and therefore how we behave. This is because it changes our perception of the world. You will begin to think about yourself differently and other people; how you handle negative situations will change; how you celebrate positive situations will change. You will feel more fulfilled and accomplished in yourself.

For some of you that have been living in an egocentric state for longer or been giving a lot more energy to these behaviours subconsciously, you will not be able to develop an open mind overnight. It may need to be a long-term goal for some of you. However, the secret to getting ahead is getting started!

You need to realise that the way you handle or think about a situation is a reflection of you and your beliefs. Most of the time, our attitude is based on the emotions we have towards a situation. Here is an example of this:

>**Situation:** An egocentric person might not like it when someone stares at them.

>**Reason**: They feel like they are being judged.

In this situation, the person may not even understand why they feel defensive towards this. This encounter is not *fact* — it has only been judged in this way based upon his emotions and triggers.

Realistically, you don't know why or what the person is staring at. It could be that they recognized them, were admiring them, or possible nothing to do with them at all — and they were simply in deep thought!

This emphasizes the importance of having control over

your emotions and being able to differentiate what you think is happening with what is actually happening. Learning to deal with this can help prevent negative thoughts or feelings you might not even understand why you have.

In time, you will be able to distinguish why a particular situation made you feel a particular way. It will help to understand the values and belief systems of other people, making you more compassionate, even if you don't believe in them. Consider this substantial self-growth!

Having a compassionate understanding moves the thoughts you have every day from → **your subconscious thinking** to → **your conscious thinking**. What this means in simple terms is that you now have become *aware*: aware of your emotions, your behaviours and your attitudes. Once you are aware of them is when you can begin to change them!

The state of consciousness that we live in day-to-day is naturally very limited as humans. It can be because we have so many distractions (such as social media) that takes up essential room in our brains. Over the years, people have discovered that there are various ways that we can free up space to reach a higher level of consciousness. These are exercises you might know of already such as meditation, yoga and other practices traditionally considered to be 'spiritual.' The reason they are becoming much more popular is because people are beginning to realise that they really do work and the results in some cases can be astonishing!

To simplify what we have learnt so far...

- Our version of reality is based upon our personal attitude and belief system. This impacts how we see a situation, person or thing.
- An attitude towards something is driven by an emotion. Therefore, our belief system is based on what we feel emotionally.

REALITY IS MADE THROUGH ACTS OF OBSERVATION AND THE CHOICES THAT OBSERVERS MAKE.

Joe Dispenza

CHAPTER 3

Perception

Joe Dispenza is a neuroscientist that specializes in things that you can do to rewire your brain. I have learnt about all of his scientific studies so that I can teach you readers how to evolve your consciousness to live a more fulfilled and happy life.

To begin with, as humans we form a group of beliefs about an idea. This can be anything — from our relationships, to what makes us angry to what brings us joy.

This group of beliefs turns into a *perception*. The definition of perception is 'the ability to become aware of something through the senses', which simply means that it is essentially a tool kit for interpreting something. The way that you interpret a situation may be different to the way someone else does; this is because you have a different perception of it based upon your beliefs.

In essence, **your perception is determined by what you think**. Your perception will never be perfect; we are proving that it is adaptable and can be changed. What this means for you is that it is very subjective and can be temporary; just because you think it is right does not mean that it is.

There are 2 realities that we live in:

The physical world
How our physical bodies work from a molecular level. This includes our genetic makeup, our biologic structure and the science behind having a human body.

The perceptive world
How our experiences are communicated to us through our senses — how we perceive touch, smell, sight and sound.

Both of these realities exist simultaneously. Dispenza says that 'we are deluded if we think that the way we see the world is how the physical world actually is' — and he isn't wrong.

We obviously know that your brain doesn't experience anything directly — even a 1° change in its temperature can leave you for dead! It has never experienced light; our perception of light is determined by electrical impulses sent to our brain via our eyes. Our perception of colour is the way in that light is reflected off different surface types.

Therefore, your perception fuels your thinking of scenarios, experiences and environments. How you saw the world previously will dictate how you see the world in the future *unless you take control of it*!

YOUR MIND
DOESN'T
EXIST IN THE
UNIVERSE;
THE UNIVERSE
EXISTS IN YOUR
MIND.

CHAPTER 4:

Quantum Physics

So, I bet you're sitting wondering, "What on earth has quantum physics got to do with me?!" Well... Quantum physics doesn't look at reality when it comes to objects. It looks at something that's called *'fields of possibility'.*

This chapter deals with things like electrons and particles, energy and atoms (all that science stuff we didn't really listen to in school!) but in a different way. We are going to realign the knowledge you probably already have and think about it in the context of *you.*

In the previous chapter, we discussed that we need to become more aware of our thoughts and behaviours and switch our thinking to become more conscious. Now, we are going to use science to prove why.

In the context of the Law of Attraction, elements of quantum physics act differently to how we know or learnt about it previously. A fundamental of physics is that **energy and matter cannot be created or destroyed**.

'Matter' is *everything* that exists in the Universe. It is defined as being every physical substance that exists or physically takes up space; it is different to mind and spirit. Energy however is quite an abstract idea, but in basic terms it's the thing that gives you the capacity to do something. You need to have energy to move, heat food, watch TV, have a hot shower.

This is all relevant, I promise!

Things come in and out of existence; animals become extinct, plants die, food expires. Whilst these things die, they don't just disappear. The matter and energy that they were made up of still exists but only in a different structure — we know this because **energy and matter cannot be created or destroyed**.

There is a lot that goes in the world that we can't see, touch or smell. Things like energy fields and creative fields exist beyond a physical reality, but just because we can't hold them doesn't mean that they are not there. You can't see the signal between the TV and the remote, but we know this electrical energy exists because *something happens*.

The results of this type of action prove that things happen around us that don't enter into our 3D world. Whilst gases are invisible, they still take up physical space (think about blowing up a balloon — how would it stay 'blown up' unless something was in it?).

The same goes for things like radiation; radiation is the movement of atoms or particles through space. Think about the electromagnetic waves that microwaves use to heat up food — you can't see it, but you can see, smell and taste its effect!

I realize that some people need a little more encouragement in believing this sort of thing, especially if it is all completely new territory for you. So here is a little extra proof...

If you have an atom — the smallest element of matter that exists — and you take it apart, it consists only of 3 physical elements; protons, neutrons and electrons (these might sound familiar from your chemistry class in school!). What it does is that the electrons orbit around the neutrons and protons (like the moon orbits the earth), and this movement is all dependent upon frequency and vibrations.

We can manifest happiness by using similar positive vibrations. This is called the Law of Attraction, but in science it is actually called the Law of Vibration. Why? Because...

Everything is energy; all energy moves and vibrates. Every thought vibrates, every thought radiates a signal, and every thought attracts a matching signal back.

Therefore, you attract what you give out.

Have you ever heard of the phrase **happy vibes**? This is where the saying comes from because vibration is literally ingrained within our biological structure and our thoughts!

RAISE YOUR VIBRATION.

Energy is not the only abstract and complex idea to exist in quantum physics, or the Universe in general. Even though it *is* of course scientific, it's not smooth, mechanical or easy to digest. Some of the most famous scientists agree that there are a lot of unanswered questions when we are talking about the Universe, but what all of the findings I have told you so far prove is that there are **so many possibilities beyond what we can see**... Vibration, energy, manifestation to name a few!

THE PAST IS A MEMORY OF AN INTERPRETATION, THE FUTURE IS A POSSIBILITY AND SPECULATION.

Yogi

CHAPTER 5:

Your Body & Your Mind

Now, let's turn to how we can use the science we have learned to elevate our minds.

When we learn something new, we literally change the structure of our brains. We create a new circuit connection — technically called a neural pathway — which allows impulses (signals from our body) to move faster around our brain. In general, it helps you learn better, think faster and can even help you stave off dementia!

However, whilst learning new things changes the physical structure of your brain, it also changes you as a person. Changing your body changes your mind.

These changes will encourage you to harness a new perception because when you change, your thoughts change. When your thoughts change, your attitudes and beliefs change. This is fundamentally what contributes to how you see the world.

This is why we say 'changing your mind' because, as you begin to think differently, your brain will restructure itself to accommodate the new, repetitive thoughts and beliefs you are having.

Many people do this subconsciously and don't even realise — has anyone ever said, "You've changed!"? Well, this is why! Old habits die hard, and the less you practise things or think about things, the sooner they are to die off in your head.

I want to help you to take advantage of this.

Your brain recognises repetition and the more you do something, the more you are likely to want to do it or genuinely think it. This is why meditation and yoga have become such a staple in everyday life for those trying to become more spiritual or have a higher sense of being.

We can use meditative techniques to help restructure our brain. The Law of Attraction works by repetitively using positive affirmations — the more you say it, the more likely you are to become it.

I *am* a magnet to money.

I *am* a powerful being.

I *am* beautiful.

I believe in *myself*.

Your brain eventually will have the hardware to be able to see new perceptions and this will create new emotional responses which will improve your experiences from this! Yes, we *actually* have the ability to control the way we see the world.

Those of you readers who are already interested in the idea of manifesting, or those of you that practise meditation regularly, would already be considered to be spiritual. This is just in the nature of the practice as it's likely that they have already helped shape your broader awareness.

Now you should be able to see that **there is science behind the hype**.

So, we now know that we have control over our experiences and that we can create new experiences in our mind. In this case, do you not think that it is possible to CREATE our ideal future? CREATE our ideal mindset? CREATE our dream life? Because at the end of the day, EVERYTHING is down to our mind set and how we see things. Our only limit is our mind.

When you sit down and think about the kind of person that you would like to become, the only thing stopping you is yourself. We can all become the idealized version we have of ourselves in our head by making a conscious effort to become it. The more that we work on our thinking and focusing on better, positive energy, we can use practices like affirmations and meditation to solidify our efforts.

It's important to use things like meditation and manifesting because it helps us become more inspired, elevated and compassionate. You might forget the reason why you're trying to better yourself and so these acts of mindfulness can bring your intentions into reality. Rather than appearing illusive, all of your efforts start to become very real and the results can begin to shine through. You will be able to see yourself becoming more selfless and less selfish.

There is a lot more than just David Elkind's research into why we are egocentric from a young age. The reason we have traits like this hard-wired into us is because our natural survival instinct empowers the ego. When this happens, your behaviour tends to become before self-orientated and egocentric because it centres all of your own desires and needs ahead of everyone else's.

However, when we are truly in the process of creation, we forget about ourselves. We use the frontal lobe of the brain which is primarily responsible for cognitive functions such as memory, emotion, impulse control, problem solving and our relationships. This helps us plan, have intent, invent and see more possibilities (of ourselves and of everything else!).

WE LIVE IN A UNIVERSE THAT RESPONDS TO WHAT WE BELIEVE.

Corbin Henry

CHAPTER 6

The Magic of Manifesting

To have outstanding results with the concepts we have talked about so far in *Beyond the Mind* and *Beyond the Eye*, we now need to put it into practise! We must use a combination of mind training and activities in our 3D reality.

As you understand a little more about the Law of Attraction and how you can connect to the Universe through vibrations, we need to reprogramme our minds to become the highest, best version of ourselves. We can experience astonishing results through manifestation because *what we put out into the Universe; we get back*.

Manifesting is to feel deep, genuine gratitude for what we

have. To manifest, we simply repeat affirmations using our outer or inner voices. Your affirmations can be any positive statement that helps you challenge and overcome self-sabotaging and negative thoughts. Once you begin to see the success of this method, it will help you start genuinely believing that the Universe can bring you the opportunity to follow your hopes and dreams.

The more work that you do on rewiring your brain to become more altruistic and less egotistic, the more compassionate and spiritual your journey will become. You need to wake up to the idea that your life is precious, and you have way more power than you ever believed before to achieve and to feel fulfilment.

The Law of Attraction is a key component in building the life that you desire; be it to have children, to make a lot of money or to buy your own house. But first and foremost, you need to understand the laws you are relying on and genuinely **believe** them. This book should have provided you with enough evidence in science and psychology to reassure that it's all *legitimate*. Knowing where these ideas come from you a deeper understanding of the laws needed to master your own life on ALL levels.

You know that 'like attracts like', and so you need to get rid of any negative thoughts, beliefs or ideas that you have and replace them with positive ones. Using affirmations will help you correct this...

If a negative thought pops into your head, **do not feed it**! Enforce your positive thinking and affirm a positive thought to replace it; you can only consciously think about one thing at a time.

Repeat it as many times as you need so that you plant the new idea in your head.

Use this strategy as often as you need. For example, if you want to attract wealth, instead of thinking 'oh no, my rent is due and I have no money', replace that by affirming and **believing** that the Universe already has its own ideas for you. Instead, say something like:

Money flows to me copiously and endlessly.

I have all the money I need.

Some of you readers might think this sounds crazy, right? But I and everyone else in the world who has manifested success will promise you that it works. Here is a little bit of my story...

In less than 12 months, I lost everything; I left a job that brought me in a high income because it was affecting me both emotionally and spiritually, and I had to file for bankruptcy. I was involved in a really damaging relationship which was not good for my mental health, physical health or general well-being. And, to top it all off, we just had the 2020 virus pandemic! This affected another job that I had because I wasn't allowed to work due to lockdown measures.

Before the coronavirus pandemic hit, I went on a trip to Thailand to find myself. I was enticed whilst I was there to become more spiritual; become a better version of myself. This made me want to act further on my intentions and explore my spirituality more.

When I got back from the trip, I decided to invest in myself; I did a lot of research, education and practised the techniques we talked about. This resulted in me finding a new romantic relationship beyond what I've ever experienced before, and I found a new path in life. I did this by redirecting my thoughts with meditation, mindfulness and manifesting what I wanted or needed, even when it looked impossible or other people doubted me.

I finally felt as though I would be able to fulfil my life for the better. Once I started to see results, I decided that it was only right for me to tell other people how to better theirs. This is when I decided to write *Beyond the* Mind and have it published.

As soon as I started to genuinely believe in these ideas is when everything started to fall into place. The higher my vibration became, the more positivity I seem to attract. I will admit that it does sound a little crazy at first, and believe me, sometimes I fall off the wagon and find myself questioning why I'm doing it. Then, something that I have been manifesting will happen and it'll remind me that I'm only human and we all have bad days. One thing I always believe in though is the Universe and **it will always look after me**!

IF YOU WANT
TO FIND THE
SECRETS OF THE
UNIVERSE, THINK
OF ENERGY,
FREQUENCY
AND VIBRATION.

Nikola Tesla

CHAPTER 7:

Enjoy Your Journey

I want to finish *Beyond the Eye* with a reflection because it is a great method in looking for ways to grow.

Take some time tonight to have a look at the night sky. Look at the stars, look at the moon… We all have a sense of wonder and we all know that everything you have seen in the sky is unparalleled in complexity and intrigue. The Universe is truly mesmerising.

The night sky can bring a sense of peace and tranquillity, but it can also make you think and realise **that there's so much more to our life than the society we get stuck in**.

Stars hold a remarkable amount of power, as does the moon and all of the other planets and elements of our solar system. The Universe that we live in is much more powerful than we choose to believe. Just like the stars that we perceive as simply little white specks in the sky — they hold so much force, unpredictability and balance. It is truly remarkable.

When you decide that you are ready to appreciate what's out there and what it represents, you will gain a much bigger understanding of your own power and that of the Universe.

Jema Fowler is a certified coach in Mindfulness, Meditation and the Law of Attraction. She has always been interested in the human mind, emotions and how they compensate one another and, through this interest, wants to help her readers heal emotional trauma and get motivated.

Beyond the Eye is the sequel to Jema's debut book *Beyond the Mind,* which is available on Amazon and all good book retailers.

For coaching, blogs and further information, please visit:

Jema_lifecoach

Jema Master Mindset Coach

www.jemalifecoach.com

Printed in Great Britain
by Amazon

67111321R00031